Close to Death

Books by Patricia Smith

Life According to Motown
Big Towns, Big Talk

Close to Death

Patricia Smith

Zoland Books
Cambridge, Massachusetts

First edition published in 1993 by
Zoland Books, Inc.
384 Huron Avenue
Cambridge, MA 02138

Copyright © 1993 by Patricia Smith

"The Boy With Beer" by Melvin Dixon, reprinted from *In the Life: A Black Gay Anthology*, edited by Joseph Beam. Copyright © 1978 by the Estate of Melvin Dixon. Reprinted by permission of the Estate of Melvin Dixon.

"Getting Your Rocks Off" by Melvin Dixon, reprinted from *In the Life: A Black Gay Anthology*, edited by Joseph Beam. Copyright © 1978 by the Estate of Melvin Dixon. Reprinted by permission of the Estate of Melvin Dixon.

FIRST EDITION

10 9 8 7 6 5 4 3 2

Book Design by Janis Owens Design
Printed in the United States of America

This book is printed on acid-free paper, and its binding materials have been chosen for strength and durability.

Library of Congress Cataloging-in-Publication Data

Smith, Patricia
    Close to death : poems / by Patricia Smith. — 1st ed.
        p.   cm.
    ISBN 0-944072-35-6
    1. Afro-American men—Poetry. I. Title.
PS3569.M537839C57 1993
811'.54—dc20   93-14215
                                                   CIP

Contents

Closer

Closest

Closed

In 1968, Martin Luther King was murdered and the West Side of Chicago exploded. Black folks — my friend Deborah, my cousin Alfonso, the taxi drivers, the busboys, the postmen, the nurses, the hustlers, the teachers, the church deacons and the pump jockeys — spilled into the streets, sparked by a rage that would not be harnessed.

Fire was a most visible fury, and it didn't take long for the world to burn. The air grew bitter with smoke that simply refused to move. The electricity had failed in my overcrowded apartment building, and tenants cowered in the gloomy halls, frightened of the erupting chaos. The bright dot of a lit cigarette would swell, someone would begin a hymn low in the throat. I was 13, the daughter of a no-nonsense, hat-wearing, God-fearing, church-going woman, so I was not allowed outside. No way.

I stood at the living room window with my trembling mother while neighbors pushed entire racks of clothing down the street, balanced cases of J & B on their shoulders, scooted past on stolen 10-speeds. Blood spurted from wounds that the wounded didn't seem to notice. Fire from the burning buildings reached for the shirt cuffs and pantlegs of daring looters. The air, now a visible thing, crept through the gaps in the window frame, bit into my eyes and tore at the lining of my throat. Even the trees on my street burned, matchsticks with their heads aflame.

Lying on a pallet on the floor that night, I watched flames lick at the sky. Bullets whizzed past my window as mothers screamed for their wayward or wounded children. "But how could the sky burn," I kept asking my mother, who was planning to sit up all night, her back against the door. "How could the sky burn?"

The next day, everything was gone. The world was a pile of rubble, whispering smoke, dotted in places by the bright color of a gym shoe, a discarded shirt, the severed head of a doll. The market where my mother haggled over the fatty cuts of meat was gone. The clothing store which once flashed cheap polyester promise from every window was gone. The dry cleaners, gone. The liquor store, gone. The shop where Motown's latest blared from every window was gone. Shards of glass sparkled on the concrete like unmined jewels. The air was so black that people on the street bumped into one another and the few buildings that were left could not be seen. Once they felt it was safe, white people — their eyes wide as saucers — drove their cars slowly through the streets of our neighborhood, gawking at the destruction like sightseers in a horrific theme park.

"Don't ever look white people in the eye," my mother instructed me firmly. "Don't speak to white people unless they speak to you first. They all think we're crazy now anyway. Don't give them any more evidence."

I listened to her. I always had. I didn't know that, more than two decades later, I would be forced to give my son a more desperate version of the same advice.

By the time my son came along, the sky had stopped burning and the sun was visible. The world hinted at possibility. I taught my son to look life in the eye, to make the world consider him on his terms. He never lowered his head for anyone. I taught him pride, the same way I taught him to read, to sing, to think, to walk.

Then Rodney King's bones were smashed beneath the repeated blows of nightsticks. The clubs whipped through the night with a sick rhythm, and the whole world was forced to watch. A schoolboy in South Africa. Martin Luther King on a balcony in Memphis. Yusef Hawkins in Bensonhurst. Rodney King clutching the dust in Los Angeles. A rage that would not be harnessed.

My son had no questions, no innnocent childhood queries like "How can the sky burn?" In each slow frame of that gritty black-and-white videotape, he saw his own future. He learned that in this strange language called American "black male" is "target." He watched as the sky caught fire again, as black people who looked just like him screamed wild enraged syllables into the faces of their captors.

So now, out of necessity, I must teach him fear. I will hate the sound of my own voice.

Yes, I taught my son to walk, but not so he could be knocked to the ground. His stride is no longer the bumbling stumble of innocence. It is the determined swagger of a young black man, a walk with its own unflappable rhythm, a walk that fights for its own life. It may protect him or kill him, but he doesn't change that walk for anyone. He slips attitude and bravado on as easily as he does his black, hooded sweatshirt. The attitude, almost a tangible mask, is to keep other people out, and to keep whatever he feels inside.

I prayed that he would never have to see the heavens catch fire. Now he moves through cold streets that bid him no welcome, walking on eggshells, burning with a fire of his own, and searching the sky for flames.

This book is for my son Damon, and for his brothers: the laborers, the inmates, the CEOs, the crack babies, the Crips, the Bloods, the students, the dropouts, the exalted and the condemned. This book is for my son Damon, and for his brothers: the elders, the griots, the preachers, the deacons, the devils, the dogs and the saints. This book is for my son Damon, and for his brothers: Brandon, Mesfen, Andre, Jason, Jules, Rodney, Richard and Ramiro. This is for my son Damon, and for his brothers: the dead, the dying, and those who chose life.

*   *   *

This book is because nearly half a million black men are behind bars in the United States. *Because I have seen my son with shackles at his ankles and wrists.* This book is because black men represent only 3.5 percent of a national college enrollment of almost 13 million. *Because I know a 51-year-old man who cannot read.* This book is because 45 percent of black males are likely to become victims of violent crime three or four times in their lifetime. *Because my father was killed by a bullet fired into the back of his head.* This book is because a black male infant born in 1993 has a 1 in 27 chance of losing his life in a homocide. *Because a gangbanger in Chicago used a 2-year-old boy as a shield.* This book is because young black men in New York City are wearing clothing emblazoned with the logo "C2D" — Close To Death. *Because so many of them are.*

C2D is a love song, an elegy, a dirge, a celebration. It is a scream, a whisper, a giggle, a sigh. It is black men everywhere, and their choices.

It is for my son Damon, who is going to make it now.
It is for my father, Otis Douglas Smith, who didn't.

My Life as a Baseball Game

by Otis Douglas Smith (1925-1977)

Friends, I stand before you now —
I'll tell you why I came;
I want to bring you a comparison
of my life and a baseball game.

I need an umpire that has known me
ever since I was born —
After searching the audience over,
I choose Sister Laney Thorns.

She is an asset to this community,
has been through stress and strife.
She may know nothing about a baseball game
But she knows this game of life.

My father passed at an early age;
he was only twenty-three.
It was then I finally realized
that he couldn't bat for me.

My mother tried, God bless her soul.
I was her only son.
But the good Lord came and got her
in 1941.

Slowly and sadly, I looked around
and I had nothing left.
I decided if I was to make it,
I had to bat for myself.

At times, I thought I couldn't make it.
My head would bow in shame.

I even tried to protest a call
and was almost thrown out of the game.

My batting average fell so low;
how bad that can make you feel.
I struck, was called out and I fouled out
and was thrown out trying to steal.

A voice spoke to me one day,
saying "In order to succeed,
just a little more faith and grace,
my brother, is all you need."

I strode up to the batting cage
knowing that I couldn't do worse.
I hit the ball between third and short,
and I ended up on first.

Ole Satan was on the mound that day;
I was standing on my Savior's word.
He threw away the ball trying to pick me off
and I went safely on to third.

I call my Savior when things look dim
and Satan gets on my trail.
Heaven and Earth can pass away,
but Jesus never fails.

I'll never be a home run king
or reach the Hall of Fame,
but none of that means as much to me
as playing in this homecoming game.

Right now I see my mother's face
and I want to shake her hand.

I hear her saying "Come on, my son"
up there in the cheering stand.

Here I'm standing on third base;
I can see the heavenly dome.
For me to get to that celestial place
I first have to make it home.

I have the same man playing on this team
that was with Daniel in the lion's den.
The race isn't given to the swift and strong,
so I have to endure to the end.

Now I'm only ninety feet from home plate,
so close that I can't turn around.
I must hurry to make it to the Promised Land;
my sun is going down.

Close

Edward or Edwin

Outside Boston City Hospital

Despite his sour smell, tangled snaps of hair,
wiry knotted beard, he looks fine. Yet he hovers
outside Emergency as if he were waiting
to be scooped up on a gurney and ushered inside.
"My name is Edward." Spies a reporter's notebook,
changes his mind: "Edwin. I'm not sick."

What the old folks used to call "blue black," Edward
sweats under three layers of prickly, matted clothing,
the top shell mostly wool. It is a July hungry for casualties.
Tattered duffle sports the worn words "Parker's Garage."
From time to time, he raises an empty plastic milk container
to his left eye, peers inside. Shakes it, looks again.
"I got a home. Ain't homeless."

A young girl, unraveled braids and laces,
tucks a baby boy away like a football,
uses her free hand to smack the one who drags behind,
saucer-eyed, sniffling, not much older than three.
"I done told you to shut up, boy, didn't I?" she hisses,
her eyes glazed and tired, her voice a child's voice.
"That's why I don't never want to take you no place.
I'm gon' kill you if you don't be quiet."
Edwin's red eyes widen.
"Leave that boy alone," he growls,
not loud enough for the girl to hear.
"Nuff killin' going on round here.
Ain't nothing but a baby yourself."

Clutching his duffle, he backs up a few steps,
dizzied by sun singing on glass and metal.
Through the windows, there is much scurrying.

"Got a brother dying in there," Edward says.
"Died two years ago.
Cancer eating up his blood,
took him on way from here."

Inside the hospital, workers and equipment move so fast
they leave behind paintbrush strokes of white and silver.
Edwin is afraid of the sick, afraid of discovering
that he is sick himself, afraid of a dark biting in his blood.
Another young girl walks by
with another baby, trembling in his blanket.
Important white men jostle the mother
as they pass. Anthony Jamal Crayton
has been shaking for two days.

Two women sit and chatter.
They are cool, polished, obviously late for work.
One munches from a bag of chips,
the other looks up now and again from a tattered paperback.
"Ain't nothing wrong with Michael, he just acting,"
The taller woman's nails are red, squared.
"Just want somebody to be feeling sorry for him.
Ain't nothing wrong with his heart 'cept I done broke
it too many times." Edwin would be reminded
of a blues lyric, would growl it crass and keyless.

But he is still on the sidewalk,
stuffing something into his duffle,
glaring at the busted zipper.
Even in the jalapeño heat,
he balances all of his home on his back,
mumbles something about going to see his brother,
peeks once again at the mysteries of the milk carton.

Edward is not sure how old he is.
"Old enough to know better," he snorts.

Asked how long he has lived in Boston,
Edwin cackles,
displaying front teeth as black as he is.
He laughs as a fly struggles in his hair.
"Girl, you's a fool. This ain't Boston. We in St. Louis."

And inside Boston City Hospital
the beds sag with dying black men,
their minds gone,
their bodies shocked by the heart's treachery,
their lives filling their chests.
And Edward won't ever come inside
to see the men in those beds wear his brother's face,
his father's face,
then his.

Terrell's Take on Things

A Saturday morning sticky as lemonade sugar,
and inside the rickety storefront that houses
Terrell's Afrocentric Barber Shop,
Fade Palace and Wild Style Emporium,
already there is the world to be dealt with.
Willie Franklin, boy from down the street —
you know, he was raised in that brick shack
right next to Fred Warren's TV repair place —
well, the boy refuse to cut that Jheri Curl
outta his head — that stuff older than free at last,
and here he come with them big oily spots all up and
down his back. Look like one of them fools trying to be
gangster, and nerve enough to have a gold tooth, too.
His foot ain't in the door hardly before Terrell starts in
on him: "Damned shame if you ask me, damned shame.
Man, it's 1993 and ain't nobody got no time
for that grease trickling down they neck,
'specially hot as it is out there. C'mere, lemme
clip that shit down, Willie. Let them naps grow out.
Couple o' weeks, I'll hook you up with a fade.
The sisters don't like putting they hands in that mess
and did y'all see that chile 'Retha onstage at the
President's thang, trailing all that fur like she
Queen 'Lizabeth and all that fat unnerneath it?
I ain't never seen no black woman with money *stay* fat.
Damn, that gal can't pass up *no* part of the chicken —
see her coming even the bones get scared.
That chile will eat a spaghetti *strap*. What that song
she sang, Ain't No Way? Well I guess it sho' ain't.
She got one chance, though — stay alive long enough,
time make you skinny. I just don't know if she got
that much time. Oh yea, oh yea, look out the window
y'all, there go that gal I was telling y'all 'bout,

got enough ass to balance a drink on. I'm gon' get
some o' that, mark my words, I'm gon' be knee deep
in that shit come Saturday night or my name
ain't Terrell Anderson Jr. and I ain't got my hand
tussling in your nappy head. Man, she don't know me yet,
but she will. I bet she done already heard 'bout how
my lovemaking done put a few sisters on crutches,
bet she done heard how I done drove one or two
outta they minds, how I whipped some o' this nature
on them and now they drooling and barking like dogs.
Hell, y'all can laugh if y'all want. Thomas, you ask
your sister. And you over there, ask yo' mama.
They say size don't matter, but it do if it's *this* size,
man. I have to bind this shit to my leg or it would
scare all y'all outta here. Come Saturday night,
you can ask that gal y'all just seen. She be passing
by that window in a wheelchair. Mark my words.

Thomas, speaking of women, one too many times
I done seen your wife over there cross the street
all up in that butcher's face, and the meat
she asking for ain't what makes it to your table
for dinner. Man, she spend all day in there, going
behind the counter like she all of a sudden
interested in the butcher business. What she interested
in is the butcher's *business* and you better start asking
yourself why. You better start taking care of stuff
at your own home, my man, 'fore she get a taste
of that sausage he selling, then you be up in here
crying about she gone, she gone. Man, I don't care
how old a woman get, you can't be taking her
for granted, climbing up on top of her poking
like you got somewhere else to be in five minutes.
And there you is, every Friday night, up in the
Continental sniffing all up Deborah Ann's young butt
like she want something from you besides that

money you always waving around. Man, anytime
you see flies buzzing around a sister and it ain't
summer, time to move on to another sister.
Damn, your wife got some nice legs on her, too,
if that butcher don't take her up on it
I might get in line. Better keep those home fires
burning man, and didn't I hear you say your
oldest boy was in the army? I sho' hope he don't
run himself into none of them sissies
Clinton trying to put in there. You know some
of them sissy boys turn you out smooth,
you never know what happened, pretty soon
you be turning your butt toward some brother
talking about go ahead baby, fill it up.
They better just keep those pretty boys
in the church choir where they belong, keep 'em
in them beauty shops and away from real men
who ain't got time for none o' that pansy stuff.
One of them chillun come in here to get his hair cut,
sitting up in my chair talking about my man this,
my man that, I just had a fight with my man.
I be scared to put my hand on the boy's scalp for
too long, scared he might start feeling all warm
and crazy. It ain't natural, it just ain't natural.
If man was meant to lay down with man, wouldn't have
to force the equipment, know what I mean?
Edward, your boy kinda fresh ain't he, I mean
he damned 40 years old and no woman
in sight. Could be he just ugly, though. Other night
I heard a blind woman turning him down, said she
could just imagine how ugly he was.
Y'all hold your horses, just keep your heads here,
I gotta pee. Now don't talk about me while I'm gone."

And Willie sit and Thomas sit and Edward sit while
inside the tiny bathroom, Terrell yells, "Pee at last,

pee at last, thank God Almighty, I'm peeing at last."
Nobody laughs. That's what he always says.

Come out with something else on his mind. "Y'all heard
'bout that boy got shot over on Madison Street the other
night? Well I heard that was John Greenley's boy
Samuel, heard he 'bout close to dying too. Hell, Lord
might strike me down, but I was scared of that boy myself,
heard he was on that crack, didn't think nothing 'bout
stealing from his mama or robbing folks on the street.
Steady talking 'bout the Vice Lords this, Vice Lords that,
like that gang he was running with meant more than his
mama or daddy. I swear man, I don't see how folks let
they kids get like that. That boy needed a few good
ass whuppings when he was little, that's all. Heard
they shot that boy in the head, that he near 'bout
blew up. Don't know what they keeping alive over in
that hospital, and I ain't seen John to ask him.
I'm just thankful I done made it this long, thankful
the Lord done seen fit to just let me make an honest
living, cuttin' some hair. Glad he leaving me here to
stir it up a little longer. And Willie, stop asking me
about that curl, talking 'bout some activator.
You need to activate your head under this razor
and lemme cut that shit outta there. This the
'90s, man, black man free now, Superfly done flew.
Been doing this 40 years. Bring that head over here."

Willie Franklin's Take on Things

Hey *chill*, Terrell. Chill.
Ain't no need to rock the house just now
with these keenly activated kinks.
Hey, Billy Dee had 'em, man. *Billy Dee.*
Man, I can *upset* some sisters
with these shiny corkscrew curls
kissing my neck. Can't help it.
And that woman who just walked by?
She busy Saturday night, man.
I should know.

So Superfly done flew, you say?
Well, I got a reason
for bopping through life
like a west side stepper,
dayglo brim tilted top the plastic bag
while the stuff I spritz
to turn this shit from bad to good
soaks like fat into my collar.

Yeah, I got a reason
for just about everything.
Notice, if you will,
the double back jump hop
in my stride. Now, both you and I know
that if black men don't strut,
the clock don't tick,
the mail don't run
and the sisters can't find a smile
to save their lives. But this hop, skip, jump
ain't 'bout nothing but survival.

These red snakeskin aero heel razor point

baddest shoes you ever saw, gleaming like plastic
and fresh outta layaway is killing these dogs.

I am full of reasons each Friday night,
real close to last call for alcohol,
using that last slow cut
to grind the Isleys
hard into some girl's jones.

But reasons come harder on Saturday morning.
Her hair's not as long,
her skin's not as light,
and she's not as much a freak as I thought.

Then, dammit, here comes that relentless bongo,
that underlying drum. My foot begins tapping
one day when I'm waiting on the Madison Street bus,
and my foot won't stop, even when
the hard plastic soles of the snakes give way.
Then it's just the bare bottoms
of my feet on concrete,
tapping crazy, and the rhythm rumbles
deep into my bones. The beginnings of pain,
but no matter,
there's something I can't get away from here,
and I know, I know,
I am destined
to eternally shake that thang.

The rhythm won't stop. Even my ass is in it.
No time to get old or nappy, man. Hell, not now.

The Room with the Star

For Little Richard

The architect of rock and roll sashays offstage,
pokes his weary veneer with a pearl-tipped hatpin
and grits his perfect teeth. The celebrated attitude
hisses from his skin, angry air from a pinched balloon.
He is left aching, cramped, nearly folded,
doubtful that the ringing cheers can spark revival,
and he waits for some hopeful, babyfaced boy diva
to take his hand, guide him past dusty backdrops
to his door, the one with the silver star.

The damned room is all light. Fat glaring bulbs
line the mirrored walls, the mirrored doors,
snicker beneath fringed shades. Lights sway from
the mirrored ceiling, dot the lazily circling 4-blade fan.
Even with his eyes shut, he is everywhere,
blotched beige in the snarling illumination,
the slick inflated pompadour glistening grease,
eyes black double-outlined and wounded.
There are too many of his mouths,
stained as a debutante's, born to pout that pretty, thank you,
never was no question. This is always where dizzy comes,
in these rooms where he cannot turn
without more of him being there, hundreds of bellies
girdled to flatness beneath rhinestone buttons,
thousands of tired bowlegs, still hiccuping with backbeat.

He'd been a god, his hair dripping venom,
Jesus, he'd played the piano with his knees, his feet,
even one kickass riff from an ambitious elbow.
He bit into microphones, chewed, crazy but helpless,
spat fillings at the jealous whores in the front row,
lost his natural mind. He took 'em to church again,

holy-rolled them till their backs cracked and left them
screaming, their hair wired and nappy, their legs waving
in the air like *cucarachas* fat on poison. He saw it begin
with the white boys loosening their ties. It always hit
them first, the ones who cackled when they first saw
his arched Vaselined brows and Georgia peach complexion,
the ones who just couldn't believe they'd plunked down
20 bucks a seat because their girlfriends wanted to see
some dusty colored queen. So he shot it into their bones,
compromised their hearts with it, threatened their spines
with a devil music that made them deny their dull, righteous
upbringing. He made them dance with their cocks in the air.
"That old black faggot got you in his spell . . .
that old black faggot thought you knew so well —"

And he got their girls too. Bent those pale little bodies back
and got that moan working right in there where it shoulda been,
leaving sweet honey-colored starfish stains
in the crotch of all those honest pink panties.
Rock done truly rolled here tonight.
Got to that point where the walls was bulging
with wicked gospel, where a room full of disciples
would have sold their souls if he'd wailed the request.
Now put *that* on a stamp. Build a shrine to that in Memphis.

They wanted a bitch, and they got one. He worked the room,
cranked the fever, screamed at the screamers to shut the fuck up.
He trilled, pranced, rolled his eyes back into his head.
Damn right, he was possessed. "*I* built this shit," he told them.
"Designed it, named it, pushed it out from between my legs."

Went on for two hours tonight, and paying for it now,
out of the spotlight, moving like an old man, an old man,
an old man, an old man, all these mirrors. Time to begin
the slow peel, glittered raiment unbuttoned, unzipped,
unsnapped, and falling. Time to free the soft belly from its

spandex cage, to ease off pointed, patent kickers.
Time to be unpretty. Fistfuls of tissue streak
with the peachy color of white women,
of young boneless boys, of Nancy Wilson.
He scrapes the eyeliner off with his finger, curses
as the black wax cakes beneath this morning's manicure.
He turns blacker, smaller. In the center of the repeating room,
weariness crooks his back and he eases himself to
the lush carpet, lying cool and broken on a pile of loud clothing.
Muzak slithers in. He is naked a million times.

Watching Buddy Guy Watch the White Boys

Forty-three seconds into the first number of the first set
and already that white boy's trapped.
Buddy, in the booth closest to the stage,
sucks his diamond-studded tooth, leans into the man's mistake
It was his job to predict this mess.
He should have known something, was wrong
when that white boy came struttin' into Legends
hauling that souped-up ax, flicking quick licks
with those skinny fingers flying,
and talking like Lincoln freed his ass.
Buddy can usually smell that shit,
send it walking before it starts to stink.
Must be getting old,
not listening the way he should.
Dizzied by those fingers,
he booked J.J. & the Jackson Blues Express,
and J.J.'s in it up to his ass now,
boxed into one of those shotgun Clapton lines
with no way out. He's trying everything, though —
gritting his teeth, whipping that long nasty hair round,
humping his crotch like that's gonna distract somebody
when his fingers fall off. Wild and tired,
the boy's looking to his drummer for help,
but there ain't but one rescue, and Buddy knows it.

Club's packed. Big kettle of chittlins
musting up the kitchen, people lining up at the
counter. Pig guts, hot sauce and blues — even bad blues —
and these folks gon' blow up. Gon' be a mess in here.
Buddy laughs out loud, and a woman with a red dress
snapped to her hips appears at his shoulder,
laughing too. At what she has no idea.
Just like magic. Buddy slips away, and people

in the room reach to touch his drooping curls,
hand him markers to scrawl "Buddy loves you"
on the overpriced T-shirts. He stops
in the middle of the bustling room,
closes his eyes and hears that white boy still riding
that kickass riff, headed for death or mercy.
J.J. can't back up, or his band will lose him.
He can't back down, 'cause Buddy's there.

Seems like they been playing all damn night,
and it's still that first song.
He can't remember asking the boy,
but he can smell Berklee, would bet on
late-night sessions at a black man's feet.

They all got it now. They watch you like a hawk,
copy you till you think you're listening to yourself.
With enough practice, anybody can get up there.
But easing out of that fire
is like easing out of a woman's body
after making love. Got to know what to do,
got to know when you're through.
And be ready to jump back in.

Damn. This ain't Buddy's regular night to play.
He likes to check out the young Turks,
down a few Buds and suck a few fatty bones, working the gristle.
But listening to that white boy search for doors
is driving him crazy. Buddy straps on
his weapon backstage, does deep-knee bends, grabs a pick.
Time to rock this boy to sleep.

That Nigga's Crazy

For Richard Pryor

The madman's heart is a disappointment,
insistent bastard gunned into required rhythms.
It no longer matters how crazy the nigga once was.
The heart, thumped ragged, sewn rigid, spitting
just enough pulse into thin line, thin line, thin line,
just enough blood into crooked forefinger.
Time to push Channel 12. Time for Tom & Jerry.
The heart flushing the face, circling the throat,
the throat scarred into twist, alternating skin and scarlet.

If only we could all find a way to portion hell
into such manageable kissings, set our faces on fire
and live to be laughed at.
Another burst of charmless ravings, and he holds
the fucking world in his fist. *I will never tell
another joke. I will lie on my back in bed forever.*
Newspapers update their obits. But the madman's heart
gets the last laugh: Boom, pop pop. Boom, pop pop.
There are mountains out there. Skinny finger pointing
repeatedly at curtained window. *Sometimes I see them.*

Gin from jelly glasses, languid baths in the arms of
well-paid strangers, horseplay with loaded pistols,
mirrors busted, chairs toppled, faces of fools slapped,
and all this while orchestrating a death so shameless,
so languid, so perfect in pitch. Just fill in the blanks.
*Richard Pryor died _____ of _____ at his home in
_____. He was _____.* And then the setting.
On the toilet? Picking his nose? With his cock buried
in an ex-wife? Perhaps a fat bullet, whizzing right
this time, stunning the heart's clockwork. Nope.
When he goes, the world's gonna bust a fuckin' gut

and that steel-tubed thumper will join in the merriment:
Boom, pop pop. Boom, pop pop. *But right now, give me*
a butter knife, a pair of scissors, anything. I'm gonna
make waves. Stop the presses, dammit. I've got a heartache.
This will be a dying like no other.
And if it's gonna be the perfect gag, timing is everything.
Boom, pop pop. Boom, pop pop. There is an art to burning.
Watch him teeter toward a conjured mountain. On fire again.

Ol' Man Johnson in the Dr. Watt Choir

"I love the Lord;
He heard my cry . . ."

It *is* another language.
It is a language knit of many skins,
a language that believes in something
it cannot see,
a language deep in the knees.

So when Ol' Man Johnson bends up from the pew,
all but nothing inside a choir robe
big enough for three souls,
Ol' Man Johnson with his fried gray hair
and blotched skin screaming 'bout 70 years,
Ol' Man Johnson, who makes sure he's there
gracing second row center *every* Sunday,
when he shoots up slow,
the thick wall of organ wail
bracing his frail back,
when Ol' Man Johnson throws his head back
and opens all of his throat,
what comes out is too strong to be just his
and too wide to be just English:

"I love the Lord;
He heard my cry . . ."

And the congregation at his back,
the men with waves in their stubborn hair,
the blubbery women tugging at their girdles,
hats heaped with real flowers,
fidgety boys in ironed polyester suits,
grandmothers with their peach-powdered wrinkles

hidden behind fluttering cardboard fans,
the organist with divinely inspired flame
at each fingertip,
the mass choir hiding its Saturday night sins
beneath a wicked side to side rock,
and Ol' Man Johnson barely closing his mouth
on the word *"cry"*
before everybody in the church
moans with all the colors in their mouths
and gives him back
just what he needs:

"I
love
the Lord . . .
He
heard
my
cry . . ."

And Ol' Man Johnson, he rocks with that answer,
and he becomes his own church,
his pomaded hair a temple of light
and long after the singing has stopped
after the Right Reverend Thomas
has saved every soul 'cept the one
on the bottom of his shoes,
Ol' Man Johnson still standing
like the antenna for the receiving of miracles,
and over the noisy collecting of quarters
his voice shakes into being,
another conversation
with the only man he's ever bowed down to.

"When I woke up this morning . . .
I said 'Thank you, Lord . . .' "

And even the quarters stop
their bright singing cause Ol' Man Johnson
has commenced to rocking.
"When I woke up this morning . . .
I said 'Thank you, Lord . . .' "

And when he leaves, it takes two men
to help him down the aisle,
full as he is of Sunday morning,
and happy as he is
'bout the Lord giving him glory
bit by bit,
and none of these folks knowing it yet,
how each week
they are helping to sing him home.

Waiting for Louis to Spill the Beans

None of them can wait to look at the body.
Earl, in his pressed cranberry suit,
pushes to the front,
leans into the burnished casket,
practically touches noses with Louis.
Lamont stands straight and stares.
He would like to weep, to scream,
to blubber, to show everyone how much
he is twisting inside, but nothing comes.
Just a smirk, a hiss. *Louis, you old bastard,*
just one more hand. The cards are waiting.
Al feels like a whale
in his pants with the popped button,
a big safety pin threatening his belly,
biting elastic on his boxers.
He always wondered what sense it made
to get dressed up for these things.
Louis wasn't gonna see,
and even if he could, he wouldn't care.
He'd just laugh that jagged heehee,
the one he couldn't stifle just before *Gin!*

Louis hardly looks dead. Head full
of crinkly silver hair, combed better
than it had ever been in life,
a little Afro-Sheen even.
Pockmarked skin a shade lighter
like he just might be dying
bit by bit, or just *thinking* 'bout dying.
But he's got on the suit he always wore to funerals,
and that strikes Al funny. He gulps a breath
to suppress the giggle, and the safety pin pops,

lances his navel. He screams, and Lamont
nods, whispers, *"Let it out, brother, let it out."*

Earl and Lamont and Al sit in the pew
behind Louis' nearly-bald wife,
his two flabby, mostly absent daughters.
One of them smells too sweet,
like an anxious hooker,
and Lamont wants to slap the backs of their heads,
all three across, Stooges style.
Since he can't cry,
he might as well raise a little hell,
give ol' Louis a heehee for the road.

The preacher starts in. From where they sit,
Al can see the tip of Louis' nose,
the stiff hand resting on his stomach, the rose.
He wonders if the body has become a shell
as the reverend moans for his money.
Al wonders if the soul has gone
north or south, or if that was just Louis,
not breathing, no heartbeat, no heehee,
destined to dust after a slow ride in midday traffic.

Earl wants the room to empty,
wants to have a word with Louis.
"C'mon old buddy, we're 71, 73, 73,
and could use the info: White light or
dark hallway? Any ex-wives around?
Is there really a judgement,
and if there is, will I go to hell
because I slapped my kid around a little,
or will Lamont be there
because he talked me into sneaking out
of a restaurant once without paying?

When my life passes in front of my eyes,
will I have to relive that moment
when I saw my little Andrew
knocked into the air by a speeding car?
What hurts, Louis, what hurts,
and what feels good? Are we talkin'
a tunnel of white light or a well of fire?
Or nothing? Damn, don't let it be nothing."

Time to view the body again. Al limps a
little. Lamont rests a hand on his shoulder.
Everyone's filing out, and Louis ain't talking.
He's just dead. And 71, 73, 73 shuffle past
then take their seats again, each one convinced
ain't nobody going nowhere without the info.
Louis, the cards are waiting.
You don't have to deal us in. Just show us your hand.

Brother Ray

For Ray Charles

Destined to become a classic?
Honey, you gon' kill me,
but you telling me what that press thing says,
and I don't know nothing 'bout that.
They could just as well say the album's
a piece of shit. You see,
here's where I get into trouble. Oh well.
I am what I am, all I'm ever gon' be;
I'm an old man, come September if I live
to see it, I'll be 63. So damned old
because I'm so set in my ways.
Nobody ever screwed around with my music.
Nobody. That ain't allowed.

I always wanted to be great,
never cared about being famous.
Like to leave something on this earth
to show I was here. Think my best music
is gon' follow me to my grave.
Can't let nobody fool with it
while I'm here, so they'll be scared to
fool with it when I'm gone.
So call me a bastard.
Talk about me behind my back.
As if I would know.

Hey, I ain't no angel. I sing ugly.
Always been nasty
in that like-it-or-lump-it way.
I rock with whatever's rolling,
and it comes from my toes,
that's where it comes from.

I'm possessed, sweetheart, by a spirit
ain't nobody got a name for.

They call me
womanizer,
abuser,
creative headache.
True, I told the world
I'd "gotten next to
many, many of the Raelettes,"
and hell, every eye ain't blind.

No matter what, always was
that pure heart singing,
and black folks always knew.
I can sing anything, any way,
and black folks will always know
what'd I say.

I ain't asking nobody to like me
or what I do. Been doing this
almost 50 years, and here are the rules:
Don't mess with me or anything I sing.
Make 'em follow the rules
and fools be sniffing round you
till you six feet under.
Don't believe me?
There's a line of white folks follow me
everywhere I go. I got 'em witchcrafted.
And those are the only folks
I don't need to see
to know they gon' *always* be there.

Us, and the World Outside

For the men of the Roxbury Men's Club

That ambulance, parked outside
the pool hall, cross the street from the projects,
third time this week. The man they stuffing inside
this time got his eyes open, but you can tell
he don't know who or where he is, or why the sun
is shining full in his face. Black boys in skullies
and Carhartts screech up on their 10-speeds
to get close, screaming *"Check this out!"*
and windows, row after row, crossways and up,
squeal in their tracks as project folks
look for something better than what's on TV.
But as drama, it hardly rates. Nothing like Tuesday
night when Deacon Miller got jacked up leaving church,
or Thursday when they found Ida Johnson's boy
face down on Shawmut Ave. That was something to see.
But this time, even the ambulance workers — skinny white boys
too damned tired to watch their backs — look bored,
their arms full of just another old nigger close to death.

Outside is what they talk about
inside the Roxbury Men's Club,
where a pool ball slides into a corner pocket.
*"They picking up that man again? Look like they
take that man outta there every two, three days."*
"He an old man?"
"Ain't no older than you. Ain't no older than you."
The ambulance still sittin' there, and just about everybody
loses interest. But some of the men in the club,
grizzled gray and accustomed to spitting teeth,
peek around the doorway, and stare.
Some draw closer, look for movement through the windows.

Nobody's talking now. Click.
Eddie pops another ball in the pocket. Smooth.

The ambulance pulls away without lights or siren.
"That mean he dead, don't it? When it leave
with no noise like that, don't it mean he dead?"
No one knows. Inside, the dozens
drown out the halfhearted games.
A sign says "POSITIVELY NO DRUGS OR DRINKING
OR PEDDLING OF STOLEN GOODS IN THIS PLACE"
but Carl teeters on the bench next to an empty
bottle of Dewar's White Label. Ol' Mike and Crazy Ty
study a checkerboard. There is much slow walking,
a bullet hole in the Coke machine. Tape across the slot.

Just a regular pool hall before they made it
private, made it membership. Now they know who
comin' in. They keep out the kids with the beepers
and puffy satin Raiders jackets, the mean ones
with crosses and Xs carved into their hair.
Any new member got to be brought in by a member.
It's a brotherhood thing. No guns or drugs,
but they deal with drinking. Drinking's legal.

Last week Eddie was robbed right on the church steps
two doors down. Young boys 'bout 10 or 12
ripped his pants right off him. Emmett tried to help,
but one pulled a gun outta his gym bag and shook it
like he was 'bout to lose his natural mind.
Emmett thought, *he just a kid, but that gun is real.*
Know he woulda used that gun.
Boy would have killed me dead
as sho' as I'm standing here talking to you.

Crazy kids ain't never had no home training,
nobody wailing on their butts

when they got smart-mouthed.
That's way it was when these men was coming up —
you did wrong, you paid, you got set straight.
A good ol' Alabama ass-whupping, good for anything
from an attitude to an evil thought.
If some of these parents had been lightin' those butts
up at home from the beginning, kids wouldn't be
out in the street now killing folks.
Rich people pass out drugs to poor black folks
and let them kill they ownself.
That's why black men dying —
they killing themselves being fools for other folks.

Sun getting carried away out there today, even
the buildings sweating, grandmothers walking slow.
So the Roxbury Men's Club men fill their cups with bitter liquid,
fire up another square,
tell their stories to each other.

Once truck drivers and sign painters,
postmen and welders, the men come to the club with the sun
and leave when Eddie closes up. Some who got a little money
tucked away drive round the block
in their Cadillacs, arms propped out the window.
They circle and circle, Shawmut to Washington, but not
much farther. Folks crazy out there.

They watch TV, see killing in the same places, over and over,
as many folks done got killed, long as it's black folks
don't seem like nobody care. Brother shot in Orchard Park,
another one shot in Grove Hall, Ida Johnson's boy,
almost Emmett. Emmett, who says *I get this feeling*
we in some kinda fishbowl. Everybody looking, but nobody
care when that fish start floating on top. Don't bother me
that we're expected to die. Everybody expected to die.
What bothers me is that nobody cares if we do.

In a lot behind the club, a garden is
fed and tended by Emmett Perry,
who's from Americus, Georgia, and good at growing things.
Cabbages, peppers, tomatoes and collards
are lined in straight rows.
Right over the fence, the base of an oak
is littered with old seats, paper, plastic cups.
While rusty-kneed children play kickball,
junkies huddle under this tree and freebase.
Emmett has tried scaring them away,
with threats, with his fist, with pleading.
He was told to mind his goddamned business.
We're back to death again.

Two women sit on milk crates
outside the club's door.
Tex, who lost an arm to a shotgun blast,
sweeps the place up when Willie tells him to.
He tells the sno-cone man that he is 64
and proud of it, peels open a brown paper bag,
unscrews the top of the bottle
and pours a drink for himself,
a drink for the ladies. The wine is bright red.
In the sun, it hurts to look at it.

*"Ain't nothin' wrong with this sweet wine if you
just know how to go with it and leave it at that."*
From inside: *"Hey Tex, is that Night Train or Wild Irish?"*
It is Wild Irish.
"Bring it on in here."
Tex does.

Closer

Reconstruction

For Rodney King

Enough of the horror. Let us consider
the delicate maze of bone in the face,
the eyes glistening and vulnerable,
teeth easily shattered. Let us wonder
at the miracles of patch and knit,
the slick immediacy of scarring,
the swelling that flattens to sinew.
Let's rejoice as human returns to human,
as new tall walking signals rebirth.

Enough of gritty reel. No more
clutching dust, curling against
metronome swing. April already,
another fire simmers. Quick,
let's find the man. Film the mending.

On the Stoop, August

Was he the only person afraid of summer?
Blue-black boys pumping distance
on the sleek skeletons of 10-speeds,
their pockets bulging with packets of Doublemint,
fat eelskin wallets; squealing children
suddenly fascinated by shards of concrete,
fast cars and balls that roll into traffic,
women with next year's thighs
folded into rubberband skirts. And was he
the only one who smelled surrender in their walk?

Did anyone else turn their back to the sun's biting?
After serving up a hello
that pops the first button on the blouse
of a woman wobbling by on too-high heels, he hisses,
"Bitch, you *could* speak."
Steam creeps up from the cracks in the sidewalk,
and yes, she could have raised her hand
and showed him the sweat on her fingers.
She could have swiveled,
made her legs longer,
licked her lips,
and swept him to the curb with the day's trash.
But she simply quickens her strut,
pretends she has much ass.
The thought of pursuing her frightens him.
Summer has a sharp edge. Anything could happen.

The resounding crack of gunshots,
anger like oil in a skillet. *Damn man,*
don't drink all my shit; pass the bottle,
pass the bottle. Scarface on somebody's box,
and behind fluttering curtains,

behind torn shades,
beneath the weeping trees,
everyone makes love.
He remembers dragging his incisors
down the ridge of a woman's back,
drawing blood, and laughing.
He remembers the moist noises.
But now all he knows is his winter body
L-folded on the stoop,
swilling bright burn from a crinkled paper cup,
and watching the boys
pumping almost upright on their bikes,
finding their rhythm and their
carved summer legs working, left, right.

Smokey Lied I

For Smokey Robinson

All of 13 years old, not only wasn't I supposed to be there, I didn't
know *how* to be there. Blue light in Michael Franklin's basement
shining off skin blotched from too many furious Clearasil rubbings,
months of trying to turn *their* skin tone into *my* skin
tone — browner than ordinary, not quite black, but black enough
that I had better have big legs to compensate. I didn't have big
legs. Double-dutch tangling didn't work the muscles in my calves,
refused to turn them into stone, so that no matter how many pairs
of sweatsocks I put on, no matter how many gobs of Vaseline I
rubbed in to make those black twigs shine like silver, I was too
black, and skinny legs on top of that.

But I was sneaking into Michael Franklin's party like I was born to
the throne, the blue bulb screwed in to suggest friction, and music
playing where men begged for everything and women found grit in
their voices. The blue bulb not blinking fast enough to hide my
hair, hotcombed into shivering strings that would nap up as soon as
I began to sweat, as *if* I was gon' begin to sweat, as *if* somebody
was gonna ask me to dance. The blue light not enough to hide
clothes that said *honey even if somebody threw a match under that child's
feet, she wouldn't know how to burn.* Clothes that said I was 13 years
old, sneaking into Michael Franklin's party, holding up that corner,
not daring to breathe, and the tiny room packed hard with bodies
and lord, what is that music saying?

Then that downbeat like the first step into hell. You know it's gon'
turn real bad later, but it's crazy warm right now. Bernard
Williams, born with dark glasses and a silver tooth in his mouth,
standing right in front of me, smelling all deep and perfect, sweet
Juicy Fruited breath on my face and for one second, just one
second, I think about running, but I know I ain't going *nowhere*. I
lift up my little arms round his neck, squeeze like the blue light

tells me to, toss him my puzzle pieces, pray for a perfect fit. His thick fingers find my ass, and I wonder if when my mama said always wear clean underwear in case of an accident if Bernard Williams was the accident she was talking about. Seventeen years old, singing in my ear and silver tooth flashing, thinking to himself she's skinny and that little bit o' hair is fried, she's still in eighth grade and too young to know any better, but Smokey is singin' ooh baby baby, and oh shit . . .

I start pretending Bernard is Smokey and that's all I need to move in his arms like an echo, like I was older and knew how to burn. Smokey *know* he's a miracle, so fine he makes your heart hurt, so fine you know you could smell behind his ears and he'd smell like cream, you could sip his bathwater through a straw. Smokey the man I wrap my arms around when ain't no man there. Smokey the man on my mind when I grind my skinny body into the full-length mirror in my room, wishing myself golden. Smokey the man tell me love can be found in the storybooks, that nappy hair and little legs don't mean nothing when a boy with good hair and green eyes decides he wants you, and Smokey the first man who begged for me just the way I was, begged in that voice like melted butter for me to stay with him, begged for me to come back, begged for me to love him the crazy way he loved me.

And suddenly Bernard Williams hair wasn't wire, but that good silk that don't catch your fingers. He wasn't black like me, but black in that milky way with skin that barely hides the blood beneath. He wasn't cracking in my ear and messing up the lyrics, but he was Smokey sweet and crying the tears of a clown, begging like he shoulda been.

Smokey dangerous that way. Turn a blue-black boy with one silver tooth and the rest of them yellow into somebody with a glass slipper and a castle in the suburbs. Smokey told me all I'd have to do is wait, that my hair would grow and wouldn't need pressing no more and would tumble around my shoulders, that the muscles in my legs would curve enough to drive a blind man crazy, that I would only be 13 once, and only for a few days. Smokey taught me the ghetto was just a state of mind, that he'd gather me up on his white horse and whisk me away to mindless days of romance where between kisses on my lips, on my shoulders, on the flat swell of my belly, he would sing, he would cry, he would beg me never to leave.

I'm all away in that daydream, all wrapped in the arms of Smoke, and Bernard Williams taking advantage of the situation, brushing me back and forth across the bulge in his pants, playing my little ass like a piano. The blue bulb's been unscrewed and all I see is shadow knotted with shadow, but I know Bernard Williams is truly black again, that that nappy hair of his could cut glass and Smokey moves back into the pocket of my heart, into the secret world of a 13-year-old girl who snuck into Michael Franklin's party and now had to find a way to peel this black panting bandage off the front of her and later explain to her mother how the crisp pink cotton underwear had gone so wrong.

Heat and Sweetness

For Mike Tyson and Desiree Washington

If I could have braided steel into my bones,
I would have. I wanted legs like tree trunks,
stone teeth with jagged edges, hammers
on the ends of my arms. I needed to know
that I could hold a woman's throat in my fist,
that she would sigh and crumple beneath my name.
That's a man you'd call champion. Not this me
with a stuttering golden smile, a chameleon's eyes.

I will be 19 forever. I will twist the necks
of men who thought they were beyond lust;
they will imagine cupping my schoolgirl ass
and screaming. All this with no help from me —
only a subdued shimmy, a whiff of heat.
And the coif must be perfect tousle,
woven in precisely over hours, human hair.
They love to tug, gather it in their hands
as I gush with feminine giggle,
scraped teeth aligned,
my thinned lips the color of roses.

Even when I was a kid, wild and all footwork,
I knew that heat was sweetness. I'd lash out
at anything or anyone until my arms burned,
until I lost sight of the big picture
and it took five grown men to pull me away
from whatever I had decided to kill.
That's what you love in me now;
you love that I smell blood in everything,
that I wear my money on my teeth,
that I don't waste time
questioning whatever confuses me.
I hit it. Watch as it goes down.

It still amazes me how easily they fall,
how I can crack their hearts across my knee
without removing a stitch.
Mere suggestion works wonders.
I have no desire to be bedded
by these money men and pretty boys —
I want Booth 1 at a few posh parties,
the rush of walking in on a famous arm,
a quick snapshot of a platonic smooch
for the sake of revelry.
But I always stop just short of crazy,
go back to playing the virgin groupie
when I feel any kind of steam.

I am uncomfortable with this new softness,
stumbling like a schoolboy over lone syllables
or whispering you the story of an icy, fairytale wife
who took a pick to my exposed heart.
The first no, and I am across from you in the ring,
massive, blacker than you first thought, ugly now.
The second *no!*, and I whistle steam,
cover you with my mouth, make you taste me.
Bitch. Cock your long legs and wish for diamonds.
Try to forget that I smell blood in everything.

I said no. Twice.
But I have never been covered by heat
that way, pinned to my back by whispers,
forced to cut short that teasing shimmy
and take it to the next phase.
I swear, there was steel braided into his bones.
He made me scream I love you, I love you,
and I had no choice but to let him
kiss me, fill me with hammers.
It would have taken five grown men
to pull him away.

Going Back Down South

Not exactly Midnight Train to Georgia, but close.
One A.M. red-eye bus to Memphis —
peppery fried chicken in a waxed bag,
six copies of *Jet*,
a scratchy blanket from home
still smelling of sex. *Viola,*
her limbs languid,
her mouth everywhere.
Outside the dust-caked window
an inky midnight ribbon unravels,
and New York City's staccato concrete boxes,
leaning in and leering windowpane teeth,
snap their goodbyes.

Pushing back in the stiff seat, he thinks
I have been defeated by a city.
It wasn't the dirt,
the homeless curling into winter commas,
or the steam wafting from boulevard grates.
It wasn't the six people bound and executed
on Valentine's Day in a shabby Bronx apartment.
It wasn't the whorish headlines in the *Post*
or the horrific rhumba when the Center blew.
It wasn't Viola, sinewy city girl,
or the way she bit into his shoulder
when she wanted him. No, it wasn't Viola
or her surrounding of him.

Last week's phone conversation
with Gra'Ma Green convinced him,
made him cram his life into soft luggage.
He could see her round wired frames
pushed down almost to dropping off her nose,

long silver hair pinned and braided,
her bony hips swimming in gingham.
"Come on home, baby," she'd cooed,
same as always,
but this time it was a dose he could swallow.
Shucking peas on her rickety porch in Memphis,
somehow the woman had known
his knotted shoulders,
heard him scream into his hands.

The Greyhound finds its rhythm. It will be days
before he buries his face in his grandmother's hair,
weeks before she will find a way
to weaken the poison in his blood. *Viola.*
Her limbs languid. Her mouth.

Super Nova Legendary

For Dorian Corey, star of "Paris Is Burning"

Harlem drag queen,
blossom-lipped walker
with fierce attitude
at the grande dame stage, honey.
Low-cut blouse, blood red,
displays monstrous cleavage,
real tits bought and paid for in '66
with her *own* money, thank you.
Sometimes I think it would be nice
to take these suckers off
for a few days.
Prone to stubble, she puts on base
just for a run to the market,
or else it's bearded and busted,
the bagboy confused.

But the balls, darling.
Back in the '60s
there was just a room full of lookers
and drag queens in showgirl gear.
But there was nothing
for the children,
nothing for the Harlem children,
the ghetto children,
and nothing at all
if you were just an ordinary queen.
Mind you, Miss Thing was *never*
an ordinary queen.

Ain't but two things wrong with this room.
I got my cigarettes. Now where's the ashtray,
and where's the fire?

Dorian Corey say everybody want to walk
can walk. The femme queens
with taffeta safety-pinned to a pout,
the butch queens with their scalps
tinged yellow from yesterday's bleaching,
butch for the ladies, who show up evil
and stay that way.
This year, though, everybody
wants to
see Madonna,
be Madonna,
smell Madonna,
everybody wants to have been gazed upon
by that knock-kneed hussy,
and Miss Dorian
could out-vogue her shameless,
didn't even need arms.

Comes with the super nova, li'l sister.
Worked a long time to jump *this* bad.
And she sashays, she struts, she levitates
and leaves the room wanting.
What's left? An ashtray, filled,
a bubbling half-glass of Pepsi,
and a cigarette butt
smelling of attitude,
stamped with her blossom-pink signature.

A Letter from Walpole Prison, 3/16/93

Sitting in my dimly lit cell
after having all my possessions
confiscated from me,
my loneliness demanded
that I disrupt my neighbor
requesting something to read.

Which, in it self is a task,
in my repressive houseing condition
to recieve anything from your neighbor
one must attach a solid object to a line
(torn sheet) and take direct aim
at the cell beside him. And hope
the line is close enough
to the two inch opening
at the bottom of your door
to retract his line
and whatever else
that might be attached to it.
Which, in this instance
happens to have been
a poem
by you.

I was real impress
with your writing.
How you was able
to relate misfortunes and
articulate it on paper.
I also enjoy writing,
not particularly poetry,
but at times I find myself

needing to express
what I am feeling
and having no other outlet
other than my pen I create stories
that have a favorable senario
which most of the time
help's ease my pain.

At this time I am indigent
and have no one that would
purchase poetry for me.

If possible,
please
send
me
poetry

Fifty Singles

He's a big man, a dacron prince,
he wears dark glasses.
He drives the wing car, eats red meat,
plays the horses.
He owns a gun, knows when to shoot it,
says all the bad words.
And he knows a woman when he sees one.

He knows a woman when he wants one,
and this one he wants.
Never mind her angles are all bad,
never mind the way streetlights shatter her hair,
the way cars screech to a scream
at the sight of her.
Never mind that she asks for money.

He's into her kicking off shoes,
her rubbing of small brown feet,
the way she inhales sidewalk
and dances to the click of neon. So he dances too.

Cause he's a bopper, a slow dragger,
he remembers Motown.
He chews the blues, sucks the Luckies,
soaks in whiskey.
He works with blades, finished grade school,
loves his mama.
He knows a hooker when he sees one.
Worse yet,
he remembers the feel of the hook.

And this lady's all business.
She has no neatly framed lies for him,

only the adjectives she uses to undress him:
big. hard. deep.

It is gentle exclamation, the way she lays him down,
the way he shuts his eyes and defines her edges
only with his hands.
It is smooth shiver, the way she closes around him.
It is much shaking.
It is soft rumbling.
It is exactly fifty dollars later.
She turns the hook in his skin.

Then he's a killer, a midnight thriller,
a real mad dog.
He's from Alabama, smokes hard city,
frayed blue collar.
He knows how much breathing will hurt later,
but he doesn't give a good goddamn.
Because he's a big man, he drives the wing car,
everything good is worth paying for
and he knows it.

Runnin' with Chuck

We never stopped long enough to realize
that we were best friends. You let me watch
as you smooched your man of the moment,
chewing on his tongue, licking his lips,
and you didn't laugh when I grimaced.
"Now you know how I feel when I think about
kissing a woman," you said. "Sick to my stomach."
I admit that I shamelessly flaunted you
as an escort, fine with your lemon color
and jet black hair, silk shirts in every shade,
no hinges in your wrists.
We hung out with Nancy Wilson,
considered drugs with Rick James,
laughed at Teddy Pendergrass' heels,
crashed the best parties,
threw our names around like they meant something.

I fell in love with you early,
imagined twisting your world to fit mine,
moving your mouth to mine one day
and having it stay there. But on our first visit
to New York, we slept in a tiny YMCA bed,
our backs touching, only my head exploding.

You took me to the bars
where the most beautiful men I'd ever seen
clamped shut when I opened the door;
you explained glory holes
and your troublesome weakness for young Puerto Ricans
and we laughed and danced and drank
and we laughed and danced and drank
and we never stopped long enough
to realize that we were best friends.

You hated my boyfriends,
blessed my writing and we lived a life
with no price tags, even though I was
a single mother, broke, and you lived in
the projects. You told my mother
that the man I'd moved in with was
a loser, and he was, but I hated you
for saying so. I imagined that you wanted me
all to yourself, without ever touching
your mouth to my throat, or wanting to.

I drove you away to Indiana and someone
exotic. You call after three long years and your voice
is so young. Send me new writing, you say, send
me your life in a package. Just like that you got me, girl.
I will kiss the envelope, knowing you will touch it.

Smokey Lied II

It was alright until Florence Ballard's heart burst in her chest. I believed you until I turned a page and found Emmett Till's bubble body, his ruptured face, until a crooked blade sliced Bernard's heart. I believed you until nightsticks whistled too close and fire scarred the sparkling streets. When a bullet shattered my father's skull, your stroking of my shoulders grew obscene. Your perfect love and sugar pleading could not bind these gaping wounds, could not convince me to wait. Wait. Wait. When I was loved, I was loved by dark men with rough fingers and no sense of music, men who had already glimpsed their own deaths. Smokey, I held your hopeful songs in my throat . . . but imagining your arms around me could no longer make me close my eyes.

Motown was mortal, battered by its own wounds, human to the point of hurting. This year in Boston, Martha Reeves, who had wailed the soundtrack to my growing, screeched and whimpered her way through "Dancing in the Streets," 20 years older than she should have been, her belly straining the zipper of a short, ugly dress of flaming chiffon. Michael Jackson scrubbed his skin with old Motown lyrics. David Ruffin and Eddie Kendrick, once silky sweet fluid, popping fingers, oiled hips and silver sharkskin, both succumbed to temptation. Berry Gordy locked himself inside the castle my pennies built for him. And Mary Wells had a box built into her throat and died before she could learn to sing again. The music was ending for all of us. And Smokey lied.

Cooley & Scoot

Too cold to be sitting out here,
full in the wind, but the TV's busted
and the world ain't nowhere else.
'Sides, Cooley be out here in a minute,
and he's always good to be clutching
a bottle of something,
ready to bust open a pack of Newports
or share a suck on his last one.
Strange where heat comes from —
it's there in a woman's tight rocking,
blasts of breathing into cupped hands,
or in a cigarette, sometimes.
I sit for a minute
and just like righteous
here come Cooley, pimping so hard
look like he trying to twist his own ankles.
Good brother, but ain't never pulled up
from the '70s. Saw "The Mack" down at
that rickety Continental movie house,
thought he seen the light
and been bigbottom pants,
aerospace kickers
and mean lean ever since.
Calling women "bitches" got Cooley shot,
lost him three teeth, half an eye
and lots of pussy, so he cut that loose in '71.
'Sides that, ain't that much changed.
The man still good for a square on a cold day,
ready with a few nickels for coffee.

Folks think Cooley crazy,
so they look around him, look over him,
push him aside while they talk their talk,

and he soaks it all in.
Cooley know more 'bout more folks
than most folks know, and right here
is where we discuss it.
From 'neath that big brim hat
Cooley see the creeping, the crying,
knows which men 'bout to tip,
and which women 'bout to be tipped on.
He knows Miss Etta's daughter
done had a white man dropping her off
every evening, and that the barber's boy
sho' been sniffing a lot lately.

Last night after gunshots
in the alley, Cooley knew who was lost
before the mama did. Knew everything
that chile was up to,
knew who pulled the trigger
when it got to be too much.

Me and Cooley on the stoop
hugging all those fat secrets,
passing them 'tween us like that last cig.
And it's always deep in the night
'fore Cooley whispers, "Night man,"
and pumps my hand. I watch him
pimping like Superfly on overdrive
right past the fools who call him fool,
humming his bass-driven theme song
and trapped in the past like he oughta be.

Nothing Pulling Him Down

Used to be all in the right briefcase,
the draping, double-breasted cut;
if the shoes glistened, nobody asked questions.
He could sit in the conference room, the boardroom,
his smile even and unchallenging,
fold himself into his chair,
work crossword puzzles in his head.
He added just the right slash of color
to the canvas, propped at attention
and as important as the flimsy paper cups,
the gently sweating pitcher of ice water,
or the coleus gushing from its brushed clay pot.
He kept those black hands flat on the table,
away from the throats of the men
who nodded tolerance when they passed him
in the halls, then struggled to keep
his hands away from his own throat.
Kept his eyes level,
his mouth shut,
and every month his bank account fattened.
Corporate magic. Used to be
that was all he asked, just to be there.

Crossing the city on the clanking train
to the brick and bricktop of the 'hood,
clicking back into brown rhythms,
his shoulders loosened, his brow smoothed.
As familiar shivered through him,
he'd slap someone if it lasted,
slam his open hand into a gabardined chest,
kick some pinkish butt, shame his peoples.
Five years of swallowing his curses,
of dimming the light behind his eyes,

of rounding out the quota,
and now he wanted something more.

Out the window, on the court,
he watches the B-Boys light fuses on their feet.
That one brother in the pocket,
eyes squeezed shut. *Stuff it*. Before the train
rumbles past, he's up again, into the air like a phoenix.
He's rocket until the train makes him memory.
All that time, nothing pulling him down.

They Say That Black People . . .

They say that black people
can't resist drums.
Not the rat a tat tat kind
not the
te te.
te te.
te. te.
that slowly guides a clueless band toward its big finish,
but those drums that feel like meat.
Those deep kettles with fat throats and battered skins,
the ones that grab a song by its short nappy hair
and growl *I* run this shit.

You wonder why fools have hit records,
why black folks are creatures of percussion,
creeping like steam into the pores
of the first available dance floor,
trapped in the thick weave of humping, pulsing and pumping,
push/pull;
you wonder why we are fools for any song with a heartbeat
or just the heartbeat alone,
not the soft hissing snare tucked neatly behind the ears of jazz,
but the kickass thump
that drives blood through a limp piece of music
to our waiting ears and from our waiting ears
to the braided bones of our spine,
and from the braided bones of the spine
to the backside,
cupped in skirt or denim,
to the backside,
to the ass
which rolls

and stutters
and chokes
and bounces
as it braces for explosion.

Dancing.

What I Would Have Told Oprah, Had She Asked

For Michael Jackson

Strange they would think I'd want to live forever.
I would like to slip these bones from my body,
lock them away in a cool room,
douse them with milk,
fold my soul quietly into one last corner.
No lights on me.

I am the edge of mirrors where no one ever looks,
the cousin who mumbles,
the first step of an idiot child.
There are a million of your arms wrapped around me,
crushing,
enclosing,
threatening my stitched road to perfect
and the tenuous braid of my body,
fingers tugging my nipples red
and brushing my startled penis.
You would kill me if I let you.
I may let you.

I sleep flat on my back,
my arms at my sides,
my eyes open,
dreaming
of kinks in my hair. I dream also of Negro women
smashing my cheek with the heels of their hands,
of scarlet fruits bursting rivers,
of dying here,
flat on my back,
arms at my sides,
my eyes open,

dreaming
of kinks in my hair.

I am just what you imagine,
a bastard zephyr cooling my own brow,
tangling in my own hair.
I am enamored of children
because I can be a toy to them.
I am enamored of Elizabeth Taylor
because she is fat and mortal.
I am afraid of my father
because he is fat and mortal.
I am fat. And mortal.

I wish I could swallow music,
feed myself with drumbeats and rainfall piano.
You would love me then. I could open my door
to all of you and all of your arms.

I know you would wrap me in stubbled linen
the color of milk,
you would batter me with your kisses,
and just before I screamed for mercy
you would scrub my filthy skin
and let me sleep.

Smokey Lied III

Meeting Smokey Robinson at South Shore Music Circus, June 1991

I almost said it. I almost —
I was this close to him. And I felt entitled to touch.
I was weary by this time,
sickened by his treachery, and that night
he had danced badly, an old man
stiffened by his deceptions,
a voice that lacked the cream I remembered.

I was this close — and he stared
at me, the skinny-legged girl
whose thighs quivered
when he hit that crystal begging,
the West Side woman
whose heart pumped when he preened
in sharkskin. I felt entitled to touch.

You lied. The words moved in my throat
and pushed at the back of my teeth. *You lied,*
you green-eyed bastard.
Life was no quick whirl on the dance floor,
brother, no sassy wink.
It was the cracking of a black man's cheek,
my first love walking away
to a jagged soundtrack.
It was blood in the air,
glass rising up in the sidewalk
to slice dancing feet, and right now
if you want to set things right,
beg me for something.

Thirteen years since I'd seen him,
and only an autograph slicing across

a black and white face to show for it —
13 years since I'd seen him,
and not even looking as he wrote it.
Man *know* he a miracle,
a real piece of work,
treating me like a fan and not a disciple.

If only he had lifted my hand to his hair,
admitted that even silk tatters,
admitted that he needed me to believe
so that we both could survive.

The blue light did not blink fast enough
to hide his lizard eyes,
and when he slid out into the night,
no rhythms lighting his way,
I was left with my arms
wrapped around myself.

Nothing Worth Saving

For Reg E. Gaines

At times, there is nothing in New York
worth saving. A man, singing "My Country
'Tis of Thee," chops off the fingers
of his dead lover, mails them to himself.
A sister, stuck in midday traffic,
is a sitting duck as a bullet
slams through her windshield.
You, my beautiful, baldheaded, blue-hot brother,
walk into a classroom
and someone in the front row
stands to challenge: "What YOU doin' here?"
A knife drops from his pocket,
careens across a polished floor.

A friend who has only met you once
calls you savior. And you're right, Reg,
I should have been with you,
I needed to see you stare
back into that kid's face,
pull in that deep, what-the-fuck breath
and say,
"Sit down, my man.
Sit down."

Up against your poetry,
nothing wrong can breathe.

Undertaker

For Floyd Williams

When a bullet enters the brain, the head explodes.
I can think of no softer warning for the mothers
who sit doubled before my desk,
knotting their smooth brown hands,
and begging, fix my boy, fix my boy.
Here's his high school picture.
And the smirking, mildly mustachioed player
in the crinkled snapshot
looks nothing like the plastic bag of boy
stored and dated in the cold room downstairs.
In the picture, he is cocky and chiseled,
clutching the world by the balls. I know the look.
Now he is flaps of cheek,
slivers of jawbone, a surprised eye,
assorted teeth, bloody tufts of napped hair.
The building blocks of my business.

So I swallow hard, turn the photo face down
and talk numbers instead. The high price
of miracles startles the still-young woman,
but she is prepared. I know that she has sold
everything she owns, that cousins and uncles
have emptied their empty bank accounts,
that she dreams of her baby
in tuxedoed satin, flawless in an open casket,
a cross or blood red rose tacked to his fingers,
his halo set at a cocky angle.
I write a figure on a piece of paper
and push it across to her
while her chest heaves with hoping.
She stares at the number, pulls in
a slow weepy breath: *"Jesus."*

But Jesus isn't on this payroll. I work alone
until the dim insistence of morning,
bent over my grisly puzzle pieces, gluing,
stitching, creating a chin with a brushstroke.
I plop glass eyes into rigid sockets,
then carve eyelids from a forearm, an inner thigh.
I plump shattered skulls, and paint the skin
to suggest warmth, an impending breath.
I reach into collapsed cavities to rescue
a tongue, an ear. Lips are never easy to recreate.

And I try not to remember the stories,
the tales the mothers must bring me
to ease their own hearts. *Oh*, they cry,
my Ronnie, my Willie, my Michael, my Chico.
It was self-defense. He was on his way home,
a dark car slowed down, they must have thought
he was someone else. He stepped between
two warring gang members at a party.
Really, he was trying to get off the streets,
trying to pull away from the crowd.
He was just trying to help a friend.
He was in the wrong place at the wrong time.
Fix my boy; he was a good boy. Make him the way he was.

But I have explored the jagged gaps
in the boy's body, smoothed the angry edges
of bulletholes. I have touched him in places
no mother knows, and I have birthed
his new face. I know he believed himself
invincible, that he most likely hissed
"Fuck you, man" before the bullets lifted him
off his feet. I try not to imagine
his swagger, his lizard-lidded gaze,
his young mother screaming into the phone.

She says she will find the money, and I know
this is the truth that fuels her, forces her
to place one foot in front of the other.
Suddenly, I want to take her down
to the chilly room, open the bag
and shake its terrible bounty onto the
gleaming steel table. I want her to see him,
to touch him, to press her lips to the flap of cheek.
The woman needs to wither, finally, and move on.

We both jump as the phone rattles in its hook.
I pray it's my wife, a bill collector, a wrong number.
But the wide, questioning silence on the other end
is too familiar. Another mother needing a miracle.
Another homeboy coming home.

Closest

A Poem for the Man Who Shot My Father

I don't know where you are now,
so for the purposes of this poem
I will imagine you dead.
The circumstances of your death,
of course,
should be ironic. A bullet smashes into
the back of your skull. A bullet
smashes into the back
of your skull. A bullet smashes into the back
of your skull. A coincidence.

For the purposes of this poem, but only
for the purposes
of this poem,
I will imagine you in hell
where you are doused and torched
each second, every second,
and you feel it all;
you feel everything.

For the purposes of this poem
I would like you to describe
my father's face
the moment he turned
and saw you
           wild-eyed and thirsty
the moment when he knew
the moment before he turned away
to run, to run

And for the purposes
of this poem, I would like to hold
that picture in my head. I would like to live

over
and
over
again
that look of an animal trapped
in the headlights

because, even though
I have imagined you dead,
you are probably not too dead to remember
that there is a hell
here too.

The Undertaker's Son

His father works with his mouth
set in a miracle,
a straight line that stays that way
even through the building of faces.
Sometimes Ricky brings his homework down
and sits in a corner of the cluttered room
that's always been too cold.
He listens more than he watches
to the grunts as his father tugs
at a stubborn triangle of flesh,
the military hum of his stitching,
the sighs when he is confronted
by a puzzle with too many pieces.

Never has his father
spoken a word,
seen a need for sentences
other than the one
laid on the soiled surface
for handiwork.

Wondering if he would ever die,
Ricky once climbed up on the table
and forced himself to stay, eyes closed,
stiff as he could. He was as tall
as Edmund Rodriguez, the kid
knifed in Carlson Park last week.
When he opened his eyes,
his father was standing there,
his mouth a perfect horrible O,
staring at his son, his own hands,
for once,
just once,
not knowing where to start.

Always in the Head

"I seen it lots of times, I seen it, just from being
on the street when something was going down;
I seen kids get killed, a few, my buddy Jules
got bucked, this gang he was down with, I mean he
wasn't even down with them when they started
beefin' with this other gang, but one day, it was hot,
I remember it was real hot, somebody called Jules
and he opened the window and looked out and
they got him in the head; you know all the
time now you got to get 'em in the head,
gotta bust that brain, man, don't shoot
'em in the head most likely they won't die,
and if they don't die you might as well kill
yourself cause soon as they can stand up
they be stalkin' you big time, man, might as well
blow yourself away. Gotta bust that brain, man.
But you know what was funny, even the folks
Jules was down with didn't know who smoked him
cause they was beefin' with so many other gangs,
and then there was Billy, they jacked him big time,
took him out just for talkin' shit, acting like he was
down with brothers who didn't even know his ass,
cocking them colors wrong, and I'm sorry for laughing,
I know the shit ain't funny, but I was still looking to
see my boys hanging in the 'hood, jiving and scoping
the bitches, but then I saw them at the wake, laid out
man, lying stiff, skin two colors too light, wearing wigs
to hold their heads on and they mamas clawing at them
and screaming out their heads for Jesus, then I knew
Jules and Billy wouldn't be hanging no more, but after
awhile you just deal with dying, you get cold with it.
It's like, 'Yo man, somebody got their cap peeled last night,

you know who it was? Man, not him man, that's foul,
he was down, man, you going to the wake? No man,
can't make it, got a game, gotta kick some ass on the court.'
You just take in the word, you know, about somebody dying
and you deal with it, can't let it twist you round and
mess your head up' cause then you let your guard down
and like I said before then you might as well kill yourself.
Me? I ain't sweatin' 'bout dying. I'm kickin' the right colors,
got my brim twisted proper. Sometimes it's even fun
hanging out at places most people are scared of,
like down at Dudley late at night, the game is not
knowing if you gon' be there when something goes down
and something always does. Somebody gets bucked and
hits the street and some folks will say 'Oh man, that's
too bad,' but almost everyone else will say 'Did you see
that guy get shot? That was live, man. Did you see how
he ran, how he fell, how he screamed like a girl?
They got him in the head, man, they *busted* that brain,
it was like the movies, man. He screamed like a fuckin' girl.' "

Tuesday, wind shakes the windows. No one is outside,
at least not that I can see, and my son pulls on
a second sweatshirt, a bulky goosedown coat. He is 15,
a year younger than Jules, a year older than the child
who saw Jules open the window
to answer to his name, to let in some air.

There are times I hate being a reporter.
I am afraid of the stories. The voices are too real,
the colors too strong.
I rewind the tape, open another computer file,
hear my son yell goodbye and slam the door
on his way out. I run to the window.
Yes. His head is covered.

The Two Boys Who Knew Jules

What they remembered between them
was almost nothing — his hair's stubborn curl,
the way the girls in the projects
could never tell if he was black or Puerto Rican.
They almost agreed on his voice.
Gruff, one said, maybe an accent.
The other one swore
it was Jules' rapidfire rap
that carved him a rep on the streets.

The two boys who knew Jules
disagree about what came before.
"Stone-cold gangbanger,
time was up before it got started."
"Nah man, he was on his own,
trying hard to straddle the line.
Jules was down man, he was down,
he was caught between."
The two boys who knew Jules
didn't know themselves yet.
So they sliced up their memories to fit,

so they wouldn't see themselves
in Jules' place. Because the two boys
who knew Jules knew one thing for sure —
someone called the name *Jules!*
The window came up and then the bullet hit,
forehead, a little to the left,
and Jules left his mark on the window,
and his mother filled the shattered frame,
cradled the half head,
and that's how the girls finally found out
that Jesus was not Puerto Rican.

Madison Street Bus, Chicago

Next stop, hell. But first, suffer the faces,
feel the pinch. A buck and a half will buy you
the choking exclamation of BBQ pits,
churches with toppled roofs,
Terrell's Afrocentric Barber Shop,
Fade Palace & Wild Style Emporium
clapping its shutters. Young men
with Xs, fists and elaborate stars
carved into their fragrant heads
climb onto the bus, ignore the fare
and sprawl in the peeling seats
as their world goes by outside.

Next stop, the Promised Land —
acres of identical little homes
with dead postage stamp yards,
grated windows and young boys
careening about like stars.
The fat Mayor Daley
promised burstings of tulips.
That American dream now flourishes
behind locked doors,
because no one dares the blacktop
that crisscrosses this
slice of the good life.
12-year-old Richard
skirting toward the screams of his mother,
bullet blew up his shoulder.

Passes the Stadium where Michael Jordan,
damn damn *damn* he play.
Like no black boy ever played.
When the Bulls clinched number 2,

Madison Street boys went downtown
and broke windows, dragged Armani
sweaters from display cases
and everybody sportin' new Nikes next day.
Damn, damn, *damn* that boy play
just like a lotta these boys play, shooting balls
through tomato crates roped to street signs.
Next stop, church. A tavern. Church. A tavern.
Next stop, hell. And every step of it, blessed.

The Dark Magicians

1993, and questions about another suicide
in a Mississippi jail. Southern trees
still dragged down by weight long relieved
and ashy brothers full of remembering
hiss old blues lyrics, ignore the spittle
on their chins. We are the river wall,
they whisper, the odd lump in summered soil.
We are the disappeared, desolate and misplaced,
dark magicians stronger than any root or conjure.
Knotting the weathered noose, we slip it down
to circle our throats, pull it to choking and jump,
our hands tied behind our backs the whole time.

The Man Who Died Tomorrow

You haven't spoken a word for years.
Your mouth twitches as if some restless thought
is struggling to get out, but all that happens
is your lips get twisted.
That's what the morning commuters see —
your twisted lips.

You have filled out forms.

All manner of voices vie for space
inside your head. You lie down on something cold.

You have begged
for room to sleep.

A man who encounters you
on his front lawn
works hard to pry your fingers open.
You square your shoulders.
He finds nothing inside the sweaty palm.
Your mouth twitches.

You have created food.

"Marvin" is scrawled on the back
of your hand in green ink.
It is there to help you remember.
It will not be among the things you have lost.

You had children. Four boys, with fire
in their moving.

There are prayers in the bags you carry.
There are no pathways through your hair.

Someone named Marvin
rides the back of your hand.

You cannot remember your father. His face.

Only you know that it was really God
you saw peddling body oils and X caps
on Blue Hill. Only you know that bones
can be heard, ticking forward like time.
Only you know that the twitching
inside your mouth is actually a song.

The lyrics escape you. You are excused.

The Train Ride

He's all brass and sawteeth,
bigger than any concrete.
Fold your face when he finds you.

He's coming straight outta
Compton, straight outta Roxbury,
straight outta South Bronx,
straight outta your tumbling sleep
and into your early morning head.
You change your seat on the train,
because he's wearing thick chains and blue leather.
His skin is too black.
He brushes too close.

Isn't that blood beneath his fingernails?
Why does he stand in the door
when there are so many seats?
Why do his pockets bulge?
Aren't you breathing harder?
Isn't the word "nigger"
rattling behind your teeth?
You're *air* to him,
and that drives you crazy,
that crawls up your back.
You can't walk the street he wears.
And now his eyes
have locked
on yours.

You're shallow showbiz,
and he's a black boy with your guts
in his teeth. Smelling smoke?
It's your smile tearing apart; it's your

"Hey, I gave ten bucks to the NAACP" smile,
and it's breaking up, breaking up while he's watching.
You can't find your breath.
You grin like a nigger in a watermelon patch.
And did he hear you think that?
Such a long way
to go; Wellesley's so far away.
Change your seat again.
Look unapproachable. Drool, mumble.

Hum something by James Brown,
or James Baldwin. Try
to keep your hands from shaking.
Shake your head when he asks for the time.
Marvel at the fact that he sounds so normal.

Must be a trick. His skin is too black.
He could kill you. They said so on television.
Shit. Where's Southie when you need it?

Newborn, July 3, 1976

Silver shaft of light, almost brutal,
and I am bending from heaven into this.
Locked into comma, first there is the
bright surprise of toes, then more of me,
uncurling, richer than what surrounds,
warm complication, and already music.

I am perfect, I am all of my fingers.
And I am black exclamation slipping
into a bleached world. Somehow I know
that this will be my color always.

In His Room. With Him Gone.

She walks into her son's room without knocking,
more a voyeur than a nurturer,
and she is knocked back, dizzied
by the thick, sour smells
that say "man."
Again, she is surrounded by the remnants
of a life lived desperately —
seven baseball caps sporting the insignia of the moment,
crumpled fast food bags,
foil packets ripped of their condoms,
posters of snarling rappers with guns in their hands
and ice in their names. She can still smell
her son, the deep musky life of him,
even though he is miles away,
anxious, shackled. The phone rings,
and it is another child with a mustache
and a roar in his throat. She could picture him
on all fours, snarling, the receiver in his teeth,
sniffing the air for her son's blood.

CRIPtic Comment

From an interview with an L.A. gang member, 1992

If we are not shooting
at someone,
then no one
can see us.

Closed

Sweet Daddy

62. You would have been 62.
I would have given you a Roosevelt Road
kinda time, an all-night jam in a
twine time joint, where you could have
taken over the mike
and crooned a couple.

The place be all blue light
and JB air
and big-legged women
giggling at the way
you spit tobacco into the sound system,
showing up some dime-store howler
with his pink car
pulled right up to the door outside.

You would have been 62.
And the smoke would have bounced
right off the top of your head,
like good preachin'.
I can see you now,
twirling those thin hips,
growling 'bout if it wasn't for bad luck
you wouldn't have no luck at all.
I said,
wasn't for bad luck,
no luck at all.

Nobody ever accused you
of walking the paradise line.
You could suck Luckies
and line your mind with rubbing alcohol
if that's what the night called for,

but Lord, you could cry foul
while B.B. growled Lucille from the jukebox;
you could dance like killing roaches
and kiss those downsouth ladies
on fatback mouths. Ooooweee, they'd say,
that sweet man sho' knows how deep my well goes.
And I bet you did, daddy,
I bet you did.

But hey, here's to just another number.
To a man who wrote poems on the back
of cocktail napkins and brought them home
to his daughter who'd written her rhymes
under blankets.
Here's to a strain on the caseload.
Here's to the fat bullet
that left its warm chamber
to find you.
Here's to the miracles
that spilled from your head
and melted into the air
like jazz.

The carpet had to be destroyed.
And your collected works
on aging, yellowed twists of napkin
can't bring you back.
B.B. wail and blue Lucille
can't bring you back.
A daughter who grew to write screams
can't bring you back.

But a room
just like this one,
which suddenly seems to fill
with the dread odors of whiskey and smoke,

can bring you here
as close as my breathing.

But the moment is hollow.
It stinks.
It stinks sweet.

The Touching of Him

For Melvin Dixon

How would he welcome the funeral of his body
and the touching, the steady touching of him?
  — Melvin Dixon, "The Boy With Beer"

He wrote at night, mostly.
Some pesky line would wake him
and he'd lie still for just a moment,
savoring the overheated skin of his lover,
thinking how tired he would be in the morning.
A legal pad, a thin-lined marker,
gallons of coffee,
and a blue night pressing at his window.
Scribbling like the gulping of air:

We ride on every naked fear you have
and discover that men like us
are not all granite, shale,
deceptive quartz, or
glittering layers of mica.

How right this felt,
shaking the lines loose,
wailing the words in solo,
a fool bracing for first sunlight.
When the smooth, metronome click
of his lover's sleep came too close,
he'd push it back by imagining the men who would
read these anxious poems — high school jocks,
Marine sergeants, giddy divas leaping with dance.
And his father, who would finally discover
that any stone glitters when the light is right.

4 A.M. The sluggish coffee biting harder
and still no end to the gospel,
no end to the furtive kisses,
jewels that glisten in dust.
My father, thin-bearded spitter of this seed,
these midnight bleedings are for you.
You will know that I have opened my mouth
upon the shoulders of men,
that I am a clattering of stones.

He cannot speak this. But when this poem
is done, his father will know how surprised
he was to wake and find a stranger
rifling through his blood. Not words this time.

The Man on the Darkie Toothpaste Box

Not only did he find something to smile about,
but his whole head grins. Top hat tilted
just so, gray bushy brows arched in jubilee,
nose widening to accommodate the glee,
glimmer circles on chocolate cheeks,
and his eyes, two amused pebbles
on rolling orbs of white, white, white.
Ears hinting wiggle, and a yassuh
at the ready. Never seen clean so clean.
Tux cocky and polished. What has he got
to smile about? We are promised
full fluoride protection, and an active ingredient
of sodium monofluorophosphate. "Cleaner teeth,
cooler taste" is the hook, but the real grabber
is that whoopee-y'all spitpolished grin,
those boxy showcase choppers. You see,
it was simply the contrast —
those pearly perfects set against
that puffed-up midnight. At their brightest.
Why not a non-threatening coon type,
gleeful about nothing at all
and chopped off at the torso?

Just a marketing ploy, a visual nudge,
subliminal seduction. Like Jemima,
his cake-flipping sistah to come,
he simply does not exist.
The moon-eyes, the bubble cheeks,

that comical straining to be happy,
mean nothing, nothing at all.
He simply is not there.

And that,

by the way,

is why

he is smiling.

Discovering Country

For Emmett Till

How giddy wide the country opened its arms to him,
giggling green from the first; feathery branches
arching above his head, blessings and sweet shade.
He could run, laughing and tripping until chest ached
and rusty bowlegs tangled; he could run
with no schoolyard bullies, storefronts or curbs
forcing his path. Whole mouthfuls of air,
smelling like free — and sidearmed stones,
always flat, kissing the river five or six times,
seven if the ripples whispered.
Even the name of this world, Greenwood,
open and fresh like sun shining in his mouth.
And everywhere, fat pods threatening juice,
fruit drooping from trees, bushes wild with roses —
nothing like Chicago, a city of gray and glass
with all its life potted in kitchenette windows,
crammed into dirty streetcorner parks.

He had the whole summer to be dazzled
by this new talk, sluggish as the river,
slurred like a radio with old batteries.
There was time to savor thick warm chunks
of buttered cornbread, paint a clown mouth
on top of his own with the juice from berries.
He slept with fresh air teasing his skin
while buzzing pressed at the screen
begging to taste him. He woke to bacon slabs
and singing. And as soon as he could,
he would begin to run, gulping difference,
until his eyes were full. He would run
that way until his mother received him in August,
blacker, gushing and bug-bitten.

And what was he to the men with pink grizzled faces,
the skinny women with cockleburrs caught in their hair?
Nothing but another boy running as fast as he could,
filling his chest with summer. He was a big boy,
brown and strong, almost to their shoulders.
No harm in whistling them a bit of city
before the last of it shook loose,
jostled by running, washed away by the river.

The buzzing rocked him that night, and any cover
was too much. His dreams were jumbled.
He was taken back to Chicago in chains.
He sang badly at the top of his lungs.
He went blind.
He pulled his stubby fingers through a woman's hair.
He dreamed that there was nothing running wouldn't solve,
and when he woke he would call his mother,
tell her that here was forever.

It was then that rough hands
pulled him from summer sleep
and men with earth in their mouths
ran with him through the moonwash,
leaving no time for bacon or gospel.

Spinning Till You Get Dizzy

For Dizzy Gillespie

It was never control we were after.
Jazz, by ragged definition,
pump-started its own heart,
sensed the possibilities of chaos
long before it became brown baby lullaby,
the ripples that pulse on the surface of whiskey.

Jazz demanded the unleashing of so many souls,
turned order into impetuous melody,
chords which blew spit at their captors,
and there was nowhere to run
and even fewer places to hide.

What gave birth to jazz,
what moist, constricted passage it struggled from,
who held it aloft,
slapped that newborn ass
and sparked the glorious screaming
doesn't matter.

What matters is fluid line shredding into scat
and us *owning* that sweetness;
what matters is cigarette-thin men
swearing at their reflections in the bartop.
What matters is sugar browns
hitching up homemade skirts
and pounding holes in the dance floor,
out past curfew and *tired* of asking the time.
What matters is the bee in the bonnet of bebop,
curses swirling from the mouth of a sax,
moans trapped in cool column of clarinet,

the blues twisting a guitar's stringed throat
and mojo rising up from the brown battered skin of drums.

There is growling in all of this,
a warning to stop and shout *hallelujah!*,
to shout praise for all that is cool and raunchy,
to be thankful for complication.
And let somebody else answer
when the disbelieving ask *Who is jazz's mama?*
What ripe woman's body curved and struggled
and pushed that hardheaded boy into the light?

And somewhere, the bell of a horn curved up.
Because, you see, it was never about control,
it was never about polished brass eking out thin notes
for maybe brown babies in sequins and hardbacked chairs.
Jazz was never capture or compliance.
It was all about the possibilities of chaos,
and he never bothered straightening that bell
cause why shouldn't heaven get the gospel too?

What he blew upset us, soured our gentle stomachs.
What did we need with music
that thrived in blue light,
music with rumbling in its feet?
We begged it go away, they banned it on the airwaves,
but the heat in our hips spoke otherwise.
Couldn't do, wouldn't do, didn't wanna do,
didn't know *how* to do without it,
those cocky, seamless blasts that rock us to rolling,
but it was not about control, it was *never* about control,
it was about the bell of a horn curved up,
not jazz's mama but her son,
all rough chin and sharkskin,
a black beret on cool kinks,

never a note to apologize for,
and
such
outrageous
cheeks.

Bathing in Blues

I am 23 years old,
only outwardly a woman,
and I twist my father's ashy, curled fingers
into a coupling with my own.
Today he forces a smile,
blinding me with a flurry of lyrics
and a flash of gold tooth.
Today he can talk
of craving something
sour and peppery for dinner,
complain halfheartedly
about the skittish TV reception,
lift a practiced, lecherous eye
at his nurses —
while the other eye is trained
on the hiccuping line
locked to his heartbeat.

After 55 years of kick and tremble,
the fat pump is not working.
It must be pulled through its motions,
each success dialed and dated,
each forced rhythm
aching for more of the same music.

But today my father billows with the blues,
crooning and cackling to drown out the clicks
of his stainless steel Jesus.
His favorite RN, an oil spill of a woman,
rumbles in, and daddy begins
growling ragged verses
of hot coffee, rocking beds,

jelly and backdoor men.
He sings loud, his eye on the line.

She smiles as she lifts his wrists
and quiets him to count the downbeats.
He squeezes his eyes shut and strains,
as if mere effort,
mere physical wanting,
entitles him to just a little more life.

But his pulse,
like the last lines of a sonnet,
refuses to scream. His heart is not working.

As he sighs and turns away
from the bitter dose of pity,
his hospital gown snags on a fold of sheet
and his calf is revealed, oddly muscled,
his thigh, gray and sinewy, and then,
like a newborn curling from sleep,
my father's penis, the flash of it there,
and before the skimpy gown is snatched down
to restore some semblance of natural order,
its soft curve is burned into my head.

And there,
with our fingers still twisted,
I imagine bathing his skin
in warm soapy water
in the days to come
when he cannot do so himself.
Lifting his body,
so much older now,
sponging away the passions,
sudsing the buttocks, pushing aside
and dabbing at crevices
unknown to most daughters.

I imagine moaning
the songs he'll no longer be able
to sing. Watching sleep
pull him away
from me.

"Girl, stop locking your eyes in on that dream —
I ain't dead yet," and I am snapped
back to this white room,
startling and antiseptic,
I am rigid with hope as the screen screams
breathe, breathe, breathe,
and my father begins to hum
along with the machine,
another bluesy verse he has no words for.
And I wish him
one static-free episode of "Lucy,"
burritos for dinner,
and a nurse with nothing to lose
before I kiss his forehead,
listen to a half-hearted verse
of "Matchbox Blues,"
and leave for my tiny apartment
where all the machines
are hidden.

Seven years later
my father will be dead,
a bullet moving him
far beyond rhythmic steel urgings
to *breathe, breathe, breathe,*
and no matter how hard I try
to recall the singing,
any naughty stanza from his throat,
I am still only outwardly a woman,
and can unearth nobody's blues
but my own.

Succumbing to Temptations

During the heyday,
cigarettes were part of the uniform.
Backstage where shimmering suits and sequinned gowns
hung in makeshift closets,
coconut hair pomade was a dressing-table fixture
and bouffant wigs teetered on styrofoam heads,
the light punctuation of a Kool completed the cool.
Smoke tangled in Diana's lashes
as she lowered them and whispered to Berry;
Marvin sucked at the stick through clenched teeth.
Li'l Stevie inhaled when he couldn't feel anyone watching,
then coughed till he cried. The keyword was cool,
and just being able to sing didn't get you there.
Damn, in the '60s *everybody* could sing,
but if you weren't cool, you weren't anywhere.

And Eddie
was cool. The focal point
of a thousand love songs,
he wound his way through the lacy lyrics
with smoky naivete, bony legs locked
in patented T-step, and the ladies in the house
go *ahhhhhhhhhhh*. There was nothing
he couldn't turn to butter. And on stage at the Regal —
Chicago South Side when it was still royal —
the Temps always came last. It would be the
Marvelettes, all moving like the letter S,
then Marvin Gaye, skinny, his eyes wild
and searching the balcony. Then Li'l Stevie Wonder,
just a little older than us, singing about grown folks' business,
and Jackie Haymon and I bet a dollar *that* boy could see.
Depending on the Saturday, James Brown might be there,
packed full of the sex we didn't want to see in our fathers,

dropping to his knees and begging
for something we hadn't even had yet.
And the Four Tops, whose growling scared us.

But we wouldn't be there unless the Temps were there,
and they always came last. I would lock my eyes
on Eddie, while Jackie pumped in her seat
for David, who moved his hips more than Elvis
and rolled his eyes back in his head
like the devil was in there working his way out.
But Eddie wrapped the arms in his voice
around me, pretend glamorous as I was
in Keds and culottes, and I went crazy like
I didn't do for anybody else except Smokey Robinson,
who was God. I swore to lose my virginity to a tenor,
but not anytime soon. Jackie swore she'd find a way
into David's dressing room, where she just *knew*
she'd find romance the way it was supposed to be.

And maybe it would have helped if he'd known
that Jackie was willing even then,
when he crumpled in that Philadelphia crack house
with no one screaming his name. And Eddie, I can still
hear you, pretty as syrup, so it's easy enough
to convince myself of this: Cool did not kill you.

The Music Swells. Fade to Black

For my father

All my life I had been writing the soundtrack
for your leaving — the music at the movie's end
when the hero pulls in a final dramatic breath.
Anyone who listened would hurt. Bells barely giggling,
the horrible sweet of trumpets, a throaty cello
threading through like a churchwoman's moan.
In college, suddenly African, I added the whispering rainstick
and the soft ping of kalimba.

And, of course, the instruments you loved
were worked in — a cheap electric guitar,
barely paid for and bursting treble,
a mournful harp for the blue overlay.
And Mahalia there somewhere, haunting, consoling,
her trembling chords a lullaby unleashed.
My composition, brave and discordant,
would become the theme music for a father's
languid storybook dying. I pictured you,
thin but Arkansas feisty,
at home in a plumped masculine bed,
no tubes jutting from your wrists,
no tremors sinking your cheek. Circled by those
who love you, but me closer than anyone,
I cupped your tiring heart
in the well of my hands,
and together we sifted memories,
chatted amicably with Death's waiting angel.
Your halo already intact,
we marveled at its shifting heat
and I'd try it on over my drooping braids
at a jaunty, unholy angle.

The music swelled
each time our skin connected.

What I know of you, daddy, can be pushed
into an imperfect paragraph. Your parents,
both dead before you'd learned to laugh.
Thirty years with your arms in vats of chocolate,
slick and sweet to the elbows. I know why
you moaned blue notes to push me into sleep.

What I know of you was written into the song
I crafted for your leaving. What I remember of you
fills my throat forever. I can sing it right now.

A Found Poem

As Far as Blood Goes
is a biographical novel that chronicles
the efforts of a talented, unhappy black youngster
to escape slavery and become a physician
(as is his natural white father).
Though the hero,
Michael Mabaya,
is fictional, his accomplishments parallel
those of hundreds of now-forgotten black men and women
who overcame the crushing barriers of their times
to lead lives of quiet achievement and dignity.

Michael Mabaya's story is the stuff of great fiction
for after he achieves his goal
and becomes a respected physician,
he draws attention to himself
by reading a controversial paper at a medical convention.

The result:
he is taken back to Virginia to be sold
as a common slave! His only hope
is that his father acknowledges him at last —
and his white brother will come to his rescue!

A Motherfucker Too

". . . the whole band would just like have an
orgasm every time Bird or Diz would play
. . . Sarah Vaughan was there also, and she's
a motherfucker too."
                              — Miles Davis

Up to you to figure out which one of 'em
we talking about. Could be any of three,
lining the babes up like dominos,
swearing they just had the love to give,
and up on stage, passing it on,
flashing it shameless, struttin' it silly,
those blowings that coulda caught fire
if fire was what they wanted.
And two of them smack slapped,
and one of them *born*
with beep beep in his blood
and even with bebopping this heavy,
it was a mess before you knew it.
Up to you to figure out
which one we talking about.
Arkansas road walking with church funk
pumping through branches and he stop
and he wail an all-night answer
the Lord don't want nothing to do with,
blue lines so funky they smelled bad.
Irrational flyer, up there so much
Gabriel post a note saying
No sidemen needed, dammit,
keep that horn in its cage.
But he blow so tender. Up baby, up,
mute like screaming through a
closed mouth. Up baby, up,
and two of them smack slapped

and one lock himself away,
riding the back of the bitch.
Strapped down on daddy's farm,
banging the walls and *shit*,
how many ways is blue?
Came out kicking, came out crazy,
and wanted nothing else but
a hungry woman after jamming.
The three of them,
dark appetites in triple,
and one stroked it out,
one exploded,
one just got old.
The thing to remember
is the collision of Miles, Bird and Dizzy,
all of them lost behind Miss V,
three motherfuckers in awe of another.

Daddy Braids My Hair, 1962

At first he rhythmed on the crown of a dust mop,
threading the tattered gray ropes under, over, through,
then under again, breaking into an uneven man beat,
weaving a thick tube that slithered loose whenever
his hands rested. I watched from our one good kitchen chair,
Sears Best gone bad, my freshly Prelled hair
as tangled as gossip and dry as straw,
a jar of sweet warm oil balanced in my lap,
a comb strong for the taming of mannish hair
wedged in my kinks, poised for that first tug.

But my father, who'd volunteered so eagerly for duty
that morning, first had to practice on the dusty
unprotesting head of a mop. I stared as he looped
the precise length over and over, sometimes lifting
his eyes to stare at the explosion atop my head,
clearly preferring the mop's droopy Caucasian strands,
its absence of mouth. By the time he was ready for me,
the fragrant hair oil had begun to cool.

He pried the comb from the tangle and his hands
hovered there like a young man above the pubic triangle
of a first lover. Thin fist gathered what it could,
and then the whining drag of the comb, popping each
nap with baby bullet sounds. Tears filled my shoulders,
made me shake. While working the oil through, he kicked in
with a low note. He was singing. How could he sing?
I didn't believe he was singing. IF YOU EVER ouch, daddy,
don't pull so hard CHANGE YOUR MIND really daddy, put some
more grease on it don't pull so hard ABOUT LEAVING,
LEAVING ME BEHIND you know what mama does daddy?
She presses it. She uses a hot comb that makes it easier
OH OH BRING IT TO ME he's singing he's singing and my

scalp's burning up BRING YOUR SWEET LOVIN' he's calling
back the mop beat, under, through, then under again,
but pulling now, pulling BRING IT ON HOME TO ME
ouch YEAH ouch YEAH ouch YEAH. And I will never
forget his wide smile, warm as butter on cornbread,
as he looked at his handiwork. So what if the
part was jagged, the braids all different lengths
of too greasy hair unraveling? We're off for ice cream,
all bowlegs and bravado and holding hands,
me showing off my shiny head to snickering Deborah Johnson,
daddy with another low song growing in his throat.

Squashed Moon

Blue Hill Ave., Roxbury, 1993

There is no God here. Only a well for screams,
a squashed moon, children with dust in their hair.
Out too late, young boys, their eyes startled
as saucers. Everything shuttered. Behind
a zippered window, an unleashed wail, a woman
curses the whiskey-colored sky. On the sides
of buildings in paint orange and teal, jagged
chalklines, switchblade scrapings — the names of
the anointed: Tico. Andre. Candyman. Dee-Black.
Too Strong. Marcus. Li'l Loco, rest in peace. Daniel.
There is no God here, only a patience for dying.
And hundreds of brick walls to exalt the dead.